Way of Beauty

Way of Beauty

Rekindling Eucharistic Amazement
through *Visio Divina*

Jem Sullivan, Ph.D.

Our Sunday Visitor
Huntington, Indiana

Nihil Obstat
Msgr. Michael Heintz, Ph.D.
Censor Librorum

Imprimatur
✠ Kevin C. Rhoades
Bishop of Fort Wayne–South Bend
December 13, 2022

Our Sunday Visitor Publishing Division
Our Sunday Visitor, Inc.
200 Noll Plaza
Huntington, IN 46750
www.osv.com
1-800-348-2440

ISBN: 978-1-63966-012-4 (Inventory No. T2751)
1. RELIGION—Christian Living—Devotional
2. RELIGION—Christian Rituals & Practice—Sacraments
3. RELIGION—Christianity—Catholic

eISBN: 978-1-63966-013-1
LCCN: 2022949312

Cover and interior design: Amanda Falk
Cover art: Jean-Auguste-Dominique Ingres, *The Virgin Adoring the Host*, c. 1852, oil on canvas, Metropolitan Museum of Art, New York.
Interior art: see Page 81

PRINTED IN THE UNITED STATES OF AMERICA

For Scott and Benedict, fellow pilgrims on the Way of Beauty

The Eucharist is the source and summit of the Christian life.

Lumen Gentium, par. 11

Contents

Introduction

I would like to rekindle this Eucharistic "amazement" …
To contemplate the face of Christ, and to contemplate it with Mary …
involves being able to recognize him wherever he manifests himself,
in his many forms of presence,
but above all in the living sacrament of his Body and his Blood.
The Church draws her life from Christ in the Eucharist;
by him she is fed and by him she is enlightened.
The Eucharist is both a mystery of faith and a "mystery of light."

John Paul II, *Ecclesia de Eucharistia*, 2003

We have been created for beauty, the visible form of truth and good-ness. God, the divine Artist, creates each human person with a profound capacity to participate in the divine life. We can do this by delighting in, standing in awe of, wondering at, and contemplating beauty, truth, and goodness. We experience beauty in God's creation, in each human person created by God, and in artistic works of human creativity. And whether we are artists or not, we experience beauty in a deeply personal way as we take up daily the task of "crafting [our] own life … to make of it a work of art, a masterpiece," as Pope St. John Paul II wrote (*Letter to Artists*, par. 2).

Our capacity for beauty leads us on a path of inner renewal as we move from the visible to the invisible mystery of God. The experience of beauty awakens our spiritual senses and prepares us for a new way of seeing the world — as "charged with the grandeur of God," in the words of the poet Gerard Manley Hopkins. Our seeing the world with the eyes of faith comes to a high point in the Eucharist, where, according to Pope Benedict XVI,

"God seeks us where we are, not so that we stay there, but so that we may come to be where he is, so that we may get beyond ourselves" (*The Spirit of the Liturgy*, 123).

To participate in the Eucharist is to experience, through its beauty and spiritual power, a deeply personal transformation of life. Just as bread and wine are changed, through the power of the Holy Spirit, into the Body and Blood of Jesus, so we who partake of the Eucharist are transformed by the same Holy Spirit into a new creation in Jesus Christ. In giving us the gift of himself as spiritual food for the journey of life, Jesus desires nothing less than our complete renewal in him. The Eucharist is Jesus' invitation to us to become his missionary disciples!

Think for a moment of the most treasured invitation you have ever received or extended to family or friends. To receive an invitation to a special gathering is a welcome delight. Perhaps the invitation comes from someone close, a family member or a friend. Or it may come as a complete surprise from an unexpected source and be received with gratitude, even astonishment. Such invitations lift us out of our ordinary routines as we think of a fitting gift to bring, an outfit to suit the occasion, and the anticipated joy of seeing and celebrating with family and friends.

Keep that treasured invitation in mind as you make this Eucharistic pilgrimage on the Way of Beauty, the *Via Pulchritudinis*, with twelve masterpieces of sacred art. Your memory of a special invitation, received or given, will help you recognize and appreciate the most profound and life-changing invitation to your own transformation that you receive whenever you attend Mass, no matter where you are on your spiritual journey: God's invitation to the sacred feast of the Eucharist!

The book you hold in your hands is a guide for your pilgrimage. Through the centuries, theologians, spiritual writers, and popes have invited us to travel on this Way of Beauty as a uniquely human and personal manner of encountering God. The goal of our journey with this book is to discover (or rediscover), through well-known masterpieces of Christian art, a sense of Eucharistic amazement as we reflect on God's loving presence and saving work at every Mass. These twelve works of art convey in color, line, movement, and form the theology, beauty, and spiritual riches of the Mass, as celebrated in the Catholic tradition. The beauty of each masterpiece is a feast for our eyes, guiding us to the beauty of the feast of the Eucharist. For, in the words of Pope Francis, "every expression of true beauty can thus be acknowledged as a path leading to an encounter with the Lord Jesus" (*Evangelii Gaudium*, par. 167).

Offered as guiding signposts for your pilgrimage on the Way of Beauty with each artistic masterpiece are passages from Sacred Scripture and the *Catechism of the Catholic Church* (CCC); prayers of the Eucharist; a brief reflection on the work of art; and a short prayer to accompany your contemplation of the sacred image. Master artists such as Rubens, Raphael, Murillo, and Ingres guide your quest to understand and respond to God's invitation to the sacred feast of the Eucharist, whether for the first time, after a long time, or as a habitual pilgrim. You may make a personal Eucharistic pilgrimage on the Way of Beauty with a journal or gather with friends, parishioners, or family to make this pilgrimage in community.

This book is meant to be a resource for *visio divina*, or "holy seeing," a spiritual practice adapted from the ancient monastic practice of *lectio divina*, or "holy reading," which is a method of contemplating Sacred Scripture. (If you wish to explore further how to adapt *lectio divina* to art appreciation, please see my 2009 book, *The Beauty of Faith: Using Christian Art to Spread Good News*.) Feel free to follow the order of the images in the book or simply choose images as you wish to contemplate them. As you journey with each sacred work of art, you can practice these steps of *visio divina*:

1. Begin with a slow "reading" of the image, taking in the main figures, events, or scene(s) depicted in the foreground and background. Let the reflection guide your "reading" of the artwork.

2. Next, silently meditate on the meaning of the symbols, composition, and story you see in light of God's word. Let the quotes from Scripture and the *Catechism* serve as a focus for your meditation.

3. Then let your meditation on the image turn to prayer as you lift your gaze from the visible to the invisible mysteries of faith. Let the prayers of the Eucharist and the *visio divina* prayers shape the prayer that arises from your heart and mind to God.

4. Finally, rest in a time of quiet contemplation of God's presence in the company of the sacred figures inhabiting the biblical or historical scene you have meditated on and prayed with. See yourself as an active participant in the stream of salvation history that reaches its high point in the Eucharist.

As you walk this pilgrimage path on the Way of Beauty, allow the many pilgrim companions gathered in this book — the artists and the sacred figures depicted in their creative works — to rekindle your Eucharistic amazement. For Jesus' promise to be with his disciples, and us, continues now in the mystery of every Eucharist, which is truly the "source and summit of the Christian life" (*Lumen Gentium*, par. 11).

1.
Sacrifice of Abel and Melchizedek

Artist unknown, c. 538–545
Basilica of San Vitale, Ravenna, Italy

Two stately Old Testament figures raise their hands to heaven as they offer their sacrifices to God. Their humble gestures of offering herald Christ's future sacrifice on the cross, the heart of the Eucharist. This mosaic by an anonymous sixth-century artist is part of an extended cycle of extraordinary Eucharistic images in the monumental Basilica of San Vitale in Ravenna, Italy. It is set in a large lunette on the south wall, close to the altar. By placing this image in proximity to the altar, the artist visually links the self-sacrifice of Jesus on the cross, the Holy Sacrifice of the Mass, and the sacrifices offered by two figures from Genesis — namely, Abel, the slain son of Adam and Eve, and Melchizedek, a warrior king and priest who lived in the time of Abraham.

The Church recalls the sacrifices of Abel and Melchizedek in the prayers of the Mass. This exquisite image reminds the faithful that the Eucharist, as the Holy Sacrifice celebrated at the altar, is a *memorial* that re-presents, or makes present, the one sacrifice of Christ. The mosaic also evokes the prayers of the presider, who, in Christ, through Christ, and with Christ, humbly offers the Church's own sacrifice of praise and thanksgiving to God.

On the left, we see the figure of Abel, whose sacrifice is recounted in Genesis 4:1–8; his name is written in bold letters above his head. He is dressed in the rustic clothing and bare sandals of a simple shepherd. His tattered tunic

In the course of time Cain brought an offering to the Lord from the fruit of the ground, while Abel, for his part, brought the fatty portion of the firstlings of his flock. The Lord looked with favor on Abel and his offering.

Genesis 4:3–4

is covered with a bright red cloak draped over his left shoulder, prefiguring both his death at the hand of his brother, Cain, and the blood of Jesus, shed on the cross. In his right hand, Abel holds aloft a fat young lamb, recalling the Genesis account of his bringing to the Lord the "fatty portion of the firstlings of his flock." Abel's sacrificial lamb prefigures Christ, the slain lamb whose unique self-sacrifice completes and fulfills, in his person, all the sacrifices of the Old Testament. Abel's lamb resonates also with the brilliant mosaic of Christ, the Lamb of God, that decorates the apse dome high above the altar of San Vitale. Behind Abel, a sturdy tree recalls the Garden of Eden, where his parents, Adam and Eve, turned away from God's love and communion. Beside the tree, a plain wooden structure foreshadows the Church that will, in the future, offer in the Eucharist a holy sacrifice of thanksgiving to God.

On the right is the priest Melchizedek, whose sacrificial offering to Abraham is recounted in Genesis 14:18–20; Melchizedek's name is also written in bold letters. A friend of Abraham and "a priest of God Most High," Melchizedek celebrated Abraham's victory in war by bringing him a sacrificial offering of bread and wine, as we will see later in Rubens's depiction of that scene. In return, Abraham gave him a tenth of all his belongings. The mosaic artist depicts the priest-king clothed in fine priestly vestments with a wide belt around his waist and an elegant cloak draped over his shoulders. The wine that Melchizedek offers is on the altar in a large, ornate, double-handled chalice. On the altar, whose cloth is decorated with an eight-pointed star, are two loaves of bread, placed on either side of the chalice. Each round piece of bread is inscribed with a cross pattern. We see Melchizedek lifting high a third piece of bread in sacrifice to God. Behind him, a church-like building alludes to the community gathered around the sacred table of word and sacrament.

Directly above the altar and the chalice of wine, we see the hand of God descending from heaven through a sky filled with swirling clouds. This crowning image in the mosaic carries up the sacrifices of Abel and Melchizedek as pleasing to God. In the same way, God accepts and blesses the gifts of bread and wine to become the Body and Blood of Jesus Christ.

To echo the theme of sacrifice, another exquisite mosaic, this one of Abraham showing hospitality to strangers and then in the act of sacrificing his son Isaac, decorates the wall across from *Sacrifice of Abel and Melchizedek*. Additionally, the best-known mosaics of the Basilica of San Vitale are those of the magnificently dressed Emperor Justinian and Empress Theodora, depicted in a Eucharistic procession and bearing a bowl of bread and a chalice of wine.

What does it mean to speak of the Eucharist as the sacrifice of the Church? The *Catechism* notes that "because it is the memorial of Christ's Passover, the Eucharist is also a sacrifice. The sacrificial character of the Eucharist is man-

By the oblation of his Body he brought the sacrifices of old to fulfillment in the reality of the Cross and, by commending himself to you for our salvation, showed himself the Priest, the Altar and the Lamb of sacrifice.

Preface V, Easter

ifested in the very words of institution: 'This is my body which is given for you,' and 'This cup which is poured out for you is the New Covenant in my blood'" (1365). In addition, the *Catechism* teaches that "the Eucharist is thus a sacrifice because it *re-presents* (makes present) the sacrifice of the cross, because it is its *memorial* and because it *applies* its fruit" (1366). Most importantly, the *Catechism* says that "in this divine sacrifice which is celebrated in the Mass, the same Christ who offered himself once in a bloody manner on the altar of the cross is contained and is offered in an *unbloody* manner" (1367, emphasis added).

The altar in *Sacrifice of Abel and Melchizedek* opens into the viewer's space. The artist invites us to take our place at this radiant table, where Jesus gives us a share in his priestly offering of spiritual worship for God's glory and the salvation of the world. The re-presentation of Jesus' sacrifice on the altar makes it possible for every Christian to be united with his self-offering, which was pleasing to God, his heavenly Father.

2.
The Meeting of Abraham and Melchizedek

Sir Peter Paul Rubens, c. 1626
National Gallery of Art, Washington, D.C.

In a scene of swirling movement, two regal figures lock eyes in a fixed gaze that marks a poignant moment in their dramatic encounter. Abraham, the muscular, bearded figure on the left, is clothed in the gold-rimmed armor of a warrior king with a sheathed sword swaying at his side. His red robe sweeps across his stately shoulders to convey movement as he steps into this meeting. We sense he is a man of earthly power, accompanied as he is by armored soldiers bearing upright spears and with serious faces framed in metal helmets. In his powerful hands, the dignified figure receives the offering of two large loaves of bread.

The gray-headed, bearded figure on the right, Melchizedek, is eager to greet and welcome his guest. A laurel wreath crowns his wispy hair, indicating his priestly and kingly role. With one hand, he gathers his fur-trimmed, gold-hued cloak around his blue garments. In the foreground, two muscular stewards carry large jugs of wine that will be part of the offering, while another steward in the background carries a large basket heavy with bread. Melchizedek's right hand extends to offer the hearty loaves to his visitor.

This remarkable scene, which resembles a tapestry, is the work of the master Flemish painter Peter Paul Rubens, celebrated among artists of the Flemish Baroque period of the sixteenth and seventeenth centuries. His sweeping, dramatic, and often large-scale scenes burst with movement, color, and physical intensity. In addition to creating altarpieces, portraits, landscapes, mythological and biblical scenes, and ancient figures, Rubens was a much sought-after designer of sketches for the active Flemish tapestry workshops of his day.

A royal commission came around 1625 for a tapestry series on *The Triumph of the Eucharist* for a Poor Clare Convent in Madrid. The tapestries would be displayed on special days of the Church's calendar, such as during Holy Week and on the feast of Corpus Christi, which celebrates the presence of the Body and Blood of Jesus in the Eucharist. In designing the tapestries, Rubens looked to paint Old Testament scenes that foreshadowed the Eucharist, such as this grand sketch of *The Meeting of Abraham and Melchizedek.*

Inspired by the Old Testament account in the fourteenth chapter of Genesis, Rubens invites us to step into the biblical scene of the momentous meeting of the priest-king Melchizedek and Abram (Abraham's name until God changed it when he made a covenant with him). The story recounts the capture of Abram's nephew,

> *Melchizedek, king of Salem, brought out bread and wine. He was a priest of God Most High. He blessed Abram with these words: "Blessed be Abram by God Most High, / the creator of heaven and earth; / And blessed be God Most High, / who delivered your foes into your hand." Then Abram gave him a tenth of everything.*
>
> Genesis 14:18–20

Lot, by four kings who had seized the lands of Sodom and Gomorrah. Abram gathered trained men of his household and went in search of his imprisoned relatives. In a night battle, Abram and his men defeated the kings and recovered the stolen goods, his nephew, and the women and children captured with him. The defeated kings came out to meet Abram. Then we are told that Melchizedek, king of Salem and priest of God Most High, brought bread and wine to Abram. He prayed a prayer of blessing on Abram and praised God, who delivered Abram's enemies into his hands. The story concludes with Abram giving Melchizedek a tenth of all his possessions (see Gn 14:17–20).

This mysterious Old Testament story of the exchange of blessings and gifts between Abram and the priest-king Melchizedek captures the ritual gestures at the heart of the Eucharist, when bread and wine are offered by the priest in memory of Jesus' words at the Last Supper and in imitation of Jesus' sacrificial offering of his body and blood on the cross. The author of the Letter to the Hebrews invokes this story in his reflection on Jesus' priesthood: "Son though he was, he learned obedience from what he suffered; and when he was made perfect, he became the source of eternal salvation for all who obey him, declared by God as high priest according to the order of Melchizedek" (Heb 5:8–10).

The meeting of Abraham and Melchizedek highlights the divine-human exchange of gifts and blessings that unfolds in the sacred encounter of the Eucharist. When we come to the sacred feast of the Eucharist, we are invited to share in Jesus' priestly mission by offering our humble and joyful spiritual worship. As the Second Vatican Council reminded the laity,

The supreme and eternal Priest, Christ Jesus, since he wills to continue his witness and service also through the laity, vivifies them in this Spirit and increasingly urges them on to every good and perfect work. For besides intimately linking them to His life and His mission, He also gives them a sharing in His priestly function of offering spiritual worship for the glory of God and the salvation of men. For this reason, the laity, dedicated to Christ and anointed by the Holy Spirit, are marvelously called and wonderfully prepared so that ever more abundant fruits of the Spirit may be produced in them. For all their works, prayers and apostolic endeavors, their ordinary married and family life, their daily occupations, their physical and mental relaxation, if carried out in the Spirit, and even the hardships of life, if patiently borne — all these become "spiritual sacrifices acceptable to God through Jesus Christ." Together with the offering of the Lord's body, they are most fittingly offered in the celebration of the Eucharist. Thus, as those everywhere who adore in holy activity, the laity consecrate the world itself to God. (*Lumen Gentium*, par. 34)

In Rubens's magnificent painting, the priest-king Melchizedek's offering of bread and wine is a compelling prefiguration of the offering of Jesus, God's High Priest. Jesus' offering of bread and wine at the Last Supper anticipated the

Be pleased to look upon these offerings with a serene and kindly countenance, and to accept them, as once you were pleased to accept the gifts of your servant Abel the just, the sacrifice of Abraham our father in faith, and the offering of your high priest Melchizedek, a holy sacrifice, a spotless victim.

Eucharistic Prayer
I, Anamnesis

sacred meal of the Eucharist as an eternal memorial of his unique and loving sacrifice on the cross. The master Baroque painter invites reflection on how our ordinary activities of daily life, unfolding in the midst of family, friends, work, and prayer, become "spiritual sacrifices acceptable to God through Jesus Christ." In this way, *all* of life prepares for and flows from the Eucharist.

VISIO DIVINA PRAYER

Heavenly Father, grant us the grace to make a daily offering to you of our lives with its joys and struggles. May we be united to the single, perfect offering of Jesus at the heart of every Eucharistic celebration.

Everything that the priesthood of the Old Covenant prefigured finds its fulfillment in Christ Jesus, the "one mediator between God and men." The Christian tradition considers Melchizedek, "priest of God Most High," as a prefiguration of the priesthood of Christ, the unique "high priest after the order of Melchizedek"; "holy, blameless, unstained," "by a single offering he has perfected for all time those who are sanctified," that is, by the unique sacrifice of the cross. (*Catechism of the Catholic Church*, 1544)

3.
The Gathering of Manna

Follower of Pieter Coecke van Elst, c. 1532–1535
Philadelphia Museum of Art

A shifting landscape of dry ground, grassy meadows, sloping hills dotted with trees, a glassy lake, and faraway mountains leads our eyes back to the distant sky overcast with clouds. From a break in the clouds we see, raining down from heaven, a shower of round white flakes of bread that fall weightlessly to the ground. In the distance, two figures raise their hands to the sky to catch the falling flakes. On the right, two men and a young child repeat the gesture, stretching their hands upward to catch the descending bread. On the left, a well-dressed figure, clothed in regal robes and with staff in hand, turns to speak to a turbaned man while pointing to the heavenly shower that covers the scene. And at the center of the composition, an elegant woman, dressed in a gold tunic wrapped in a delicate white robe, kneels while gazing up at the sky as a few pieces of bread fall onto the tray she holds in her right hand.

The anonymous creator of this painting was a student of Pieter Coecke van Elst, the renowned sixteenth-century Flemish court painter, sculptor, architect, and designer of stained glass and tapestries. The artist invites us to step into the miraculous scene recounted in the sixteenth chapter of Exodus. As the people of Israel wander in the wilderness, they begin to grumble to Moses and Aaron. At the heart of their discontent is a longing for the

food they ate while en-
slaved in Egypt. Moses
reminds them that their
grumbling is, in fact, a
complaint against God!
Then, hearing the peo-
ple's cry, God responds
to their hunger by prom-
ising to feed them with
meat and bread for the
rest of their journey. Moses tells Aaron to invite
the people to come close
to the Lord, who has
heard their complaints.
And as Aaron speaks to

the whole assembly of Israel, the glory of the Lord appears in the clouds.
Moses, shown here with staff in hand, converses with the people on the
Lord's behalf and delivers God's promise, saying, "In the evening twilight
you will eat meat, and in the morning you will have your fill of bread, and
then you will know that I, the LORD, am your God" (v. 12).

From the beginning, God desired to remain close to the creatures he
created in and for love. This divine desire for communion with creatures
was well known to the people of Israel. Throughout their history, the Israelites were given many concrete assurances of the divine closeness and the
providential care of God. The commandments of the law were received as
guideposts for living in covenant relationship with God. Then came nu-
merous signs and miracles, each more wondrous than the last, by which
God rescued the Israelites from captivity in Egypt. Despite their many in-

*In the evening, quail
came up and covered the
camp. In the morning
there was a layer of dew
all about the camp, and
when the layer of dew
evaporated, fine flakes
were on the surface of the
wilderness, fine flakes like
hoarfrost on the ground.
On seeing it, the Israelites
asked one another, "What
is this?" for they did not
know what it was. But
Moses told them, "It is
the bread which the* LORD
has given you to eat."

Exodus 16:13–15

You are indeed Holy,
O Lord, the fount
of all holiness.

Make holy, therefore,
these gifts, we pray,

by sending down your
Spirit upon them
like the dewfall,

so that they may
become for us

the Body and Blood of
our Lord Jesus Christ.

Eucharistic Prayer II,
Thanksgiving and Epiclesis

fidelities in the form of idolatry and grumbling against God, the people of God were never left wanting or abandoned in the desert. As they made their long, difficult passage through the wilderness to the promised land, God provided, constantly and abundantly, for their daily needs for food, shelter, and protection, nourishing them with meat and with bread in the form of manna. God fed the Israelites not once or twice, but every day of their journey! Sustaining them every step of the way was the divine gift of food and drink they needed to survive the dangerous trek through the desert.

God's generosity and closeness to the people of Israel continues to the present day in the age of the Church in the gift and power of the Holy Spirit. At every Eucharistic blessing, the priest prays to God to sanctify the gifts by sending down the Holy Spirit, like dewfall, on the bread and wine so they will become for us the Body and Blood of Jesus. In the Eucharist, we encounter the ancient desire of God to feed and nourish us on the journey of life. Jesus gives us the spiritual food of his own Body and Blood in the sacramental signs of bread and wine of the Eucharist. When we eat this bread and drink this cup, God's own loving hand feeds and strengthens us on our earthly pilgrimage.

Here, the artist offers a poignant, visual reminder of God's intense, on-going desire to feed the people with spiritual food. We see Moses alerting Aaron to the miracle unfolding before them. And as the lively figures in the painting look up to gather the manna falling from heaven, they receive, with gratitude, God's loving care in the form of bread for each day of their demanding journey. They direct our gaze heavenward to see, with faith, that God feeds us daily with spiritual food at the table of the Eucharist, where Jesus' loving sacrifice on the cross becomes divine spiritual food for our daily journey of life.

VISIO DIVINA PRAYER

Holy Spirit, grant us eyes of faith to see your powerful presence, coming down like dewfall, in the miracle of bread and wine that becomes the sacramental presence of Jesus in the Eucharist.

In the Old Covenant bread and wine were offered in sacrifice among the first fruits of the earth as a sign of grateful acknowledgment to the Creator. But they also received a new significance in the context of the Exodus: the unleavened bread that Israel eats every year at Passover commemorates the haste of the departure that liberated them from Egypt, the remembrance of the manna in the desert will always recall to Israel that it lives by the bread of the Word of God, their daily bread is the fruit of the promised land, the pledge of God's faithfulness to his promises. … When Jesus instituted the Eucharist, he gave a new and definitive meaning to the blessing of the bread and the cup. (*Catechism of the Catholic Church*, 1334)

4.

The Holy Family at Table

Artist unknown, Spanish, 17th century
Philadelphia Museum of Art

The family meal table offers a unique opportunity for the sharing of food, drink, and the joys and burdens of daily life. In our age, dominated by screen time, the experience of enjoying food and conversation together around a family table is an antidote to the depersonalization of life by technology. When a family, the basic cell of society, shares nourishment and the ordinary experiences of life, the bonds of intimacy and mutual trust grow.

For most of his earthly life, Jesus experienced living in a family, sharing the condition of most of humanity. In the ordinary, daily activities of the home in Nazareth with his mother, Mary, and his foster father, Joseph, Jesus partook in meals, work, and the intimate closeness of their family relationships. It is this daily life in the school of love of the Holy Family that an anonymous, seventeenth-century Spanish painter captures for our contemplation. The image is an invitation to take our place at the dining table in their humble home in Nazareth. There we glimpse how a simple meal shared by the Holy Family points to the sacred meal of the Eucharist, celebrated by the family of the Church.

The artist places the Holy Family in a bare room filled with simple furniture, illustrating their poverty. In the background, a large kitchen cupboard with three drawers provides a platform for a series of plates of vary-

*When they had fulfilled
all the prescriptions
of the law of the Lord,
they returned to Galilee,
to their own town of
Nazareth. The child
grew and became strong,
filled with wisdom;
and the favor of God
was upon him.*

Luke 2:39–40

ing sizes and shapes. Two bowls of different sizes on either end help to balance the backdrop.

On the left, Mary is seated at the table with her hands folded in prayer as she inclines her haloed head toward her divine Son, Jesus. Her red and blue robes signify the humanity and divinity of the Child she bore into the world. He is the second Person of the Blessed Trinity, and she turns to look at him with eyes of faith as his mother and his first disciple. Her head, covered in a silken white veil, reflects a warm golden light that illuminates the room and evokes her contemplative spirit; for as Saint Luke tells us, from the moment of Jesus' birth in Bethlehem and the visit of the shepherds who came in haste to adore her newborn Son, Mary "kept all these things, reflecting on them in her heart" (Lk 2:19). Both Mary and Joseph had the unique privilege of watching Jesus grow in strength, wisdom, and the favor of God.

On the right, Joseph, also with haloed head, lifts his folded hands in a strong gesture of prayer. Joseph responded to God's call to care for Jesus and Mary, and he showed his fatherly love with utmost humility, courage, and gentleness. In depicting Joseph in the ordinary clothes of a carpenter, the artist highlights the quiet strength and simplicity of the man God chose to be the foster father of Jesus, guardian of the Redeemer of the world. Joseph's bearded, wrinkled face expresses his awe and wonder at God's plan, unfolding in the daily company of Jesus and Mary. Beneath the curtain draped around his frame, a cat stretches out to get his attention, pointing to the ordinariness of domestic life around this family meal.

Joseph's life was centered on God's word. He set aside his own plans to put God's word first. With courage born of grace, Joseph accepted God's word as true and said yes to God's providential plan for his role in salvation history. As the husband of Mary and the foster father of Jesus, Joseph was nourished daily at the sacred feast of Jesus' presence in their home in Nazareth.

Various rich foods grace this family table, covered in white linen. From fruit to bread, meat, fish, cheese, and other delicacies, it seems that a generous feast was prepared and served for this family meal. On a smaller table in the foreground, the artist has painted a glass of red wine, a ceramic jug, and a wine flask wrapped in a woven basket.

At the center of this family meal is the Child Jesus. He is clothed in a simple tunic of red, a color that foreshadows his sacrifice on the cross and

Look, O Lord, upon the Sacrifice which you yourself have provided for your Church, and grant in your loving kindness to all who partake of this one Bread and one Chalice that, gathered into one body by the Holy Spirit, they may truly become a living sacrifice in Christ to the praise of your glory.

Eucharistic Prayer
IV, Epiclesis

VISIO DIVINA PRAYER

Jesus, grant us the grace to recognize your extraordinary presence in the ordinary, even routine, moments of daily life in our communities and homes.

The hidden life at Nazareth allows everyone to enter into fellowship with Jesus by the most ordinary events of daily life. (*Catechism of the Catholic Church*, 533)

links visually to the Eucharistic wine in the glass directly before him. His haloed head radiates divine light, and his eyes look up to heaven in thanksgiving to his heavenly Father. Jesus' right hand is raised to bless the bread in front of him and on the plates of Mary and Joseph. As this family meal unfolds, Jesus anticipates his last meal on the night before his death on the cross, when he will institute the Eucharist for the family of the Church.

When Jesus shared ordinary family meals with Mary and Joseph, he learned obedience to the commandments and to God's will. In the school of love that was the Holy Family, Jesus was prepared for the moment of his Passover from life to death to new life. In the home at Nazareth, Jesus grew in his desire to share himself as spiritual food and drink for the journey of life with all who come to the sacred meal of the Eucharist.

5.
The Marriage Feast at Cana

Bartolomé Esteban Murillo, c. 1672
The Barber Institute of Fine Arts, Birmingham, United Kingdom

A crowd of exuberant guests gathers around a newly married couple seated at the finely decorated table of their wedding feast. Sumptuous foods, wine glasses, and a richly decorated wedding cake convey the generous hospitality of the hosts, who keep the ancient customs of a Jewish wedding banquet. Servers in the background carry large plates of food, indicating that the feast is at its height. The excitement of the guests is palpable as they move with delight while speaking animatedly in the elegant room, draped with a sweeping curtain above the couple's heads. A group of figures on the left fix their gaze on the beautiful bride, who is dressed in an ornate wedding gown and bedecked with jewels and flowers in her chestnut hair. On the right, guests gaze intently at the turbaned bridegroom, seated at the center of the painting in a lavish, gold-trimmed blue robe. A little child peers out playfully between the bride and groom.

We sense that the seventeenth-century Spanish Baroque painter Bartolomé Esteban Murillo has captured a dramatic moment at this wedding feast: The bride and her parents are downcast with humiliation at the lack of wine as the eyes of some in the room turn toward them. The groom is aware of their embarrassment as he focuses on two special guests seated at the outer left of the table: Jesus and his mother, Mary, who accepted the

invitation to this wedding feast in Cana, as recounted in the second chapter of the Gospel of John. Their presence transforms this wedding celebration into an extraordinary display of Jesus' miraculous power that affirms the plan of God for the beauty and dignity of marriage.

Jesus' presence also brings a distinctive Eucharistic dimension to this wedding feast, for in this first of Jesus' public signs, revealing his divine identity and mission, his presence at this table anticipates the table of his Last Supper. At that sacred Passover meal, Jesus would institute the Eucharist for all times and all people, establishing the earthly liturgy in which the faithful on earth participate in the eternal and heavenly liturgy. Murillo invites us into this Gospel scene so that we, too, can be witnesses to the astonishing miracle unfolding before our eyes.

On the far left, behind an ornate metal decanter, Mary turns her haloed, veiled head to draw the attention of her divine Son to the empty wine jars. Jesus' mother is attentive to the practical needs of this couple as they face the shame of running out of wine at their wedding feast. She comes to their help by bringing their real, human need to the attention of Jesus. The mother's faith in her divine Son opens the way for his power to be revealed. For just as Mary interceded for this couple, she continually points out the needs of humanity to her Son. As the Mother of God and the Mother of the Church, Mary is our spir-

On the third day there was a wedding in Cana in Galilee, and the mother of Jesus was there. Jesus and his disciples were also invited to the wedding. When the wine ran short, the mother of Jesus said to him, "They have no wine." [And] Jesus said to her, "Woman, how does your concern affect me? My hour has not yet come." His mother said to the servers, "Do whatever he tells you." … Jesus told them, "Fill the jars with water." So they filled them to the brim. Then he told them, "Draw some out now and take it to the headwaiter." … The headwaiter called the bridegroom and said to him, "Everyone serves good wine first, and then when people have drunk freely, an inferior one; but you have kept the good wine until now." Jesus did this as the beginning of his signs in Cana in Galilee and so revealed his glory, and his disciples began to believe in him.

John 2:1–11

Blessed are you, Lord God of all creation, for through your goodness we have received the wine we offer you, fruit of the vine and work of human hands, it will become our spiritual drink.

Preparation of the
Altar and the Offerings

itual mother, too!

At Mary's plea on behalf of the couple, Jesus' divine power is manifested before all. Jesus, strong and stately, is dressed in a regal robe of blue. His head radiates divine light, and his face is bathed in the warm shaft of light that emanates from the upper left corner of the room. With his right hand, he points to six stone water jars, typically used in Jewish ceremonial washings. Jesus' face turns toward the group of waiters who have just heard the words of Mary: "Do whatever he tells you." A young boy watches in amazement as a waiter pours water, while a steward looks in astonishment at Jesus. A small dog, a symbol of fidelity, sits at Jesus' feet. The corner lines of the floor tile and a single raised step direct our gaze to Jesus' extended hand, a visual reminder of his divine power to change water into wine.

The master painter Murillo beckons us into this remarkable scene through line, light, movement, and composition. His expressive painting is an invitation to take our place at this wedding feast, which foreshadows the Eucharist as a transformation for our spiritual nourishment and unity as a community of faith. As we respond to the divine invitation, we discover that our needs, both great and small, are transformed in the superabundance of divine generosity unfolding at every sacred banquet of the Eucharist.

VISIO DIVINA PRAYER

Jesus, grant us true faith in the intercession of Mary, your mother, whom you gave to us to be a trusted companion on the Way of Beauty. May we trust that Mary will bring our every human need to you, her divine Son.

The sign of water turned into wine at Cana already announces the hour of Jesus' glorification. It makes manifest the fulfillment of the wedding feast in the Father's kingdom, where the faithful will drink the new wine that has become the Blood of Christ. (*Catechism of the Catholic Church*, 1335)

6.
The Parable of the Prodigal Son

Bartolomé Esteban Murillo, c. 1667–1670
National Gallery of Art, Washington, D.C.

Jesus told the parable of the prodigal son to the scribes and Pharisees who complained that he welcomed sinners, eating with them freely. The return of sinners to God was the divine reason for Jesus' life, death, and resurrection. Every day of Jesus' life revealed, in one way or another, the love and mercy of his heavenly Father and his desire to reconcile humanity to God. To open the eyes of the scribes and Pharisees to his divine identity and mission, Jesus, the master Teacher, used each detail in the parable of the prodigal son to demonstrate the love of God, whose mercies never end.

In this remarkable painting, titled *The Return of the Prodigal Son*, Bartolomé Esteban Murillo delivers an evocative visual homily that allows us to contemplate the details of this familiar parable. Using the artistic device of a "simultaneous narrative," Murillo places together multiple moments of the parable in one scene to lead our eyes around the painting as it carries us into the heart of Jesus' story: an invitation to return to the Lord from those far places we may have wandered to.

As we read the painting from left to right, the parable unfolds before our eyes. On the left, a young boy, beside a man carrying an ax, leads a fatted calf. They have been told by the father to prepare a lavish feast that this household will enjoy as they celebrate the return of the long-lost son.

So he got up and went back to his father. While he was still a long way off, his father caught sight of him, and was filled with compassion. He ran to his son, embraced him, and kissed him. His son said to him, "Father, I have sinned against heaven and against you; I no longer deserve to be called your son." But his father ordered his servants, "Quickly bring the finest robe and put it on him; put a ring on his finger and sandals on his feet. Take the fattened calf and slaughter it. Then let us celebrate with a feast, because this son of mine was dead, and has come to life again; he was lost, and has been found." Then the celebration began. Now the older son had been out in the field and, on his way back, as he neared the house, he heard the sound of music and dancing. … He became angry, and when he refused to enter the house, his father came out and pleaded with him. … He said to him, "My son, you are here with me always; everything I have is yours. But now we must celebrate and rejoice, because your brother was dead and has come to life again; he was lost and has been found."

Luke 15:20–32

On the right, a steward, dressed in bright yellow, bears a tray piled with fine clothes and sandals, while a second servant holds up a ring. These are symbols of the restored dignity and place of the prodigal son, once lost through a squandered life but now recovered in the heart of this family. In the shadow on the outer right, we see the older son looking on intently, displeased at this turn of events. Like the scribes and Pharisees, he is blinded by self-righteousness and fails to recognize the amazing in-breaking of divine grace in the repentance and return of his wayward brother to the family.

While these details capture the background elements of the story, Murillo holds our gaze on the center of the composition. There, we see the prodigal son and his father in a tender embrace. The son kneels before his father, his eyes raised in hope, his hands tightly clenched as he begs for forgiveness. His clothes are torn and tattered, his feet gnarled and coated with dirt. In his wanton state, the prodigal son is a symbol of humanity, separated from God in self-seeking sin and pride.

Jumping up to greet its returning master is the family pet, a little white dog, a symbol of fidelity and devotion.

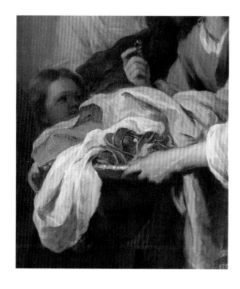

Amid the flurry of the family activities, our eyes rest on the gentle, bearded figure at the center of the scene — the loving, joyful father, clothed in generous robes of red and blue, who stoops to welcome his returning son into the embrace of his arms and the love of his family. A warm, golden light illuminates the father's wrinkled hands, which convey his tender mercy and forgiveness as he rejoices, saying, "This son of mine was dead, and has come to life again; he was lost, and has been found" (Lk 15:24).

God is love. In this extraordinary parable, Jesus paints with words what it means to be loved by God and to be, in turn, an instrument of God's love in the world. Murillo's eloquent painting serves as a reminder that when we return to the Lord, we encounter, again and again, a God who is rich in mercy and forgiveness. This tender image invites us to respond to Jesus' call to conversion, penance, and renewal of life, which is at the heart of Christian discipleship.

As he did during his earthly life and at the Last Supper, Jesus has continued to eat and drink with sinners in every age of the Church, even today. When we accept his invitation to the sacred feast of his Body and Blood, we who are sinners begin our participation in the Eucharist by acknowledging

I confess to almighty God and to you, my brothers and sisters, that I have greatly sinned

in my thoughts and in my words, in what I have done, and in what I have failed to do;

through my fault, through my fault, through my most grievous fault;

therefore I ask blessed Mary ever-Virgin, all the Angels and Saints,

and you, my brothers and sisters, to pray for me to the Lord our God.

Confiteor, Penitential Act

VISIO DIVINA PRAYER

Holy Spirit, open the ears of our hearts to hear Jesus' gentle call to receive divine forgiveness and merciful love as we pray "Lord, have mercy" at Mass.

Christ's call to conversion continues to resound in the lives of Christians. This *second conversion* is an uninterrupted task for the whole Church who, "clasping sinners to her bosom, [is] at once holy and always in need of purification, [and] follows constantly the path of penance and renewal." This endeavor of conversion is not just a human work. It is the movement of a "contrite heart," drawn and moved by grace to respond to the merciful love of God who loved us first. (*Catechism of the Catholic Church*, 1428)

our sinfulness. Asking the prayers of Mary, Mother of God, the angels, the saints, and our brothers and sisters, we pray, "I confess to Almighty God …" Then we beg humbly for God's forgiveness as we pray, "Lord, have mercy; Christ, have mercy; Lord, have mercy." Each time we pray these words, we are welcomed back to the table of the Lord with the tender embrace of our loving Father, who rejoices to see his lost children come to new life again.

7.
The Last Supper

Juan de Juanes, c. 1562
Museo del Prado, Madrid

At Passover, the people of Israel remember and celebrate their passing over from slavery in Egypt to freedom and a covenant relationship with God, as recounted in the Book of Exodus. By celebrating the Last Supper with his apostles during a Passover meal, Jesus showed the meaning of his suffering, death, and resurrection, when he would pass over from life to death to new life with God, his heavenly Father. Jesus desired that his disciples, and we too, would share in his divine life of grace and peace. So he invites us to the sacred table of the Eucharist, the memorial of his new Passover, anticipated at the Last Supper.

In *The Last Supper*, Juan de Juanes, master Spanish Renaissance artist, offers for our contemplation the solemn moment when Jesus institutes both the Eucharist and the priesthood on the night before his death on the cross. Influenced by Raphael and Leonardo da Vinci, the artist completed this altarpiece for the Church of San Esteban in Valencia, Spain, sometime between 1555 and 1562. In his evocative rendering, he offers a compelling visual catechesis on the sacred event of the Last Supper. As we follow the dramatic movements and lively expressions of each of the Twelve Apostles, we find our place at this sacred table, at which Jesus instituted the Eucharist as the enduring sign of his loving self-gift on the cross.

A long table covered in white linen spans the darkened room, framed by green curtains and an arched window that opens out onto a distant landscape. Half-eaten loaves of bread, a few used knives, a gleaming, half-empty glass decanter of wine, and a large, bare metal serving plate indicate that this Passover meal has begun. On the patterned tile floor in the foreground, the artist has placed a large brass jug and basin to recall Jesus' humble gesture of washing the feet of his disciples. Some of the disciples' feet are visible under the table — including those of the one who will soon betray him. Foreshadowing the divine humility of the cross, Jesus showed the path of servant discipleship when he said: "You call me 'teacher' and 'master,' and rightly so, for indeed I am. If I, therefore, the master and teacher, have washed your feet, you ought to wash one another's feet. I have given you a model to follow, so that as I have done for you, you should also do" (Jn 13:13–15). Jesus instituted the priesthood so his disciples could become living icons of his presence in the world.

From left to right, we see the Twelve Apostles, their haloed heads framed by their names, moving animatedly with

When the day of the feast of Unleavened Bread arrived, the day for sacrificing the Passover lamb, [Jesus] sent out Peter and John, instructing them, "Go and make preparations for us to eat the Passover." When the hour came, he took his place at table with the apostles. Then he took the bread, said the blessing, broke it, and gave it to them, saying, "This is my body, which will be given for you; do this in memory of me." And likewise the cup after they had eaten, saying, "This cup is the new covenant in my blood, which will be shed for you. And yet behold, the hand of the one who is to betray me is with me on the table." And they began to debate among themselves who among them would do such a deed.

Luke 22:7–8, 14, 19–21, 23

For when the hour had come for him to be glorified by you, Father most holy, having loved his own who were in the world, he loved them to the end; and while they were at supper, he took bread, blessed and broke it, and gave it to his disciples, saying: Take this, all of you, and eat of it, for this is my Body, which will be given up for you.

Eucharistic Prayer IV, Institution Narrative

gestures of worship, praise, and adoration. On the left, Thaddeus (Jude) clasps his hands in fervent prayer, while Matthew and Bartholomew raise their hands in awe, and James the Elder rests his left hand on the table. Peter and Andrew press close to Jesus in rapt contemplation of this gift of faith. On the right, John and Thomas are steeped in prayerful meditation, while James the Younger points their gaze to the elevated Host. Simon and Philip mirror Matthew's and Bartholomew's gestures with hands raised in wondrous delight. In Eucharistic amazement, each apostle contemplates the blessed bread that Jesus raises in his right hand, a visual connection to the sacred Host of the Eucharist. At the center of the composition, we see the serene, bearded figure of Jesus, clothed in robes of sacrificial red and royal purple, his haloed head framed by the open window. On the table in front of him is a chalice of wine, and with his right hand, he raises the blessed bread as he says, "This is my body, which will be given for you; do this in memory of me."

The sharp contrast between divine love and human sinfulness unfolds at this meal. For even as Jesus institutes the Eucharist as an everlasting memorial of his suffering and death on the cross, the worst of human betrayal manifests itself. On the outer right side of the table sits Judas, clothed in eye-catching yellow and slyly

concealing a moneybag with his right hand. His twisted posture expresses the greed and infidelity that twist his heart and mind toward betrayal. His name is etched on his seat, and his head is the only one that does not bear a halo. His sin is among the basest of human temptations — namely, to betray his master, friend, and Lord for a few earthly pieces of silver.

Juan de Juanes provides a visual catechesis on the Last Supper, inviting us to contemplate the origin of the Eucharist. Faithful to Jesus' command, the Church continues to do, in his memory, what he did on the eve of his suffering and death on the cross. And we are invited, in this repeatable sacrament of initiation, to take our place at the table of the Eucharist. There, Jesus nourishes us on the journey of our spiritual life with nothing less than the spiritual food of his own Body and Blood.

VISIO DIVINA PRAYER

Jesus, as we receive your sacred Body and Blood in the Sacrament of the Eucharist that you instituted, may our lives be transformed so we become what we receive: your Body and Blood offered for the world.

The Lord, having loved those who were his own, loved them to the end. Knowing that the hour had come to leave this world and return to the Father, in the course of a meal he washed their feet and gave them the commandment of love. In order to leave them a pledge of this love, in order never to depart from his own and to make them sharers in his Passover, he instituted the Eucharist as the memorial of his death and Resurrection, and commanded his apostles to celebrate it until his return; "thereby he constituted them priests of the New Testament." (*Catechism of the Catholic Church*, 1337)

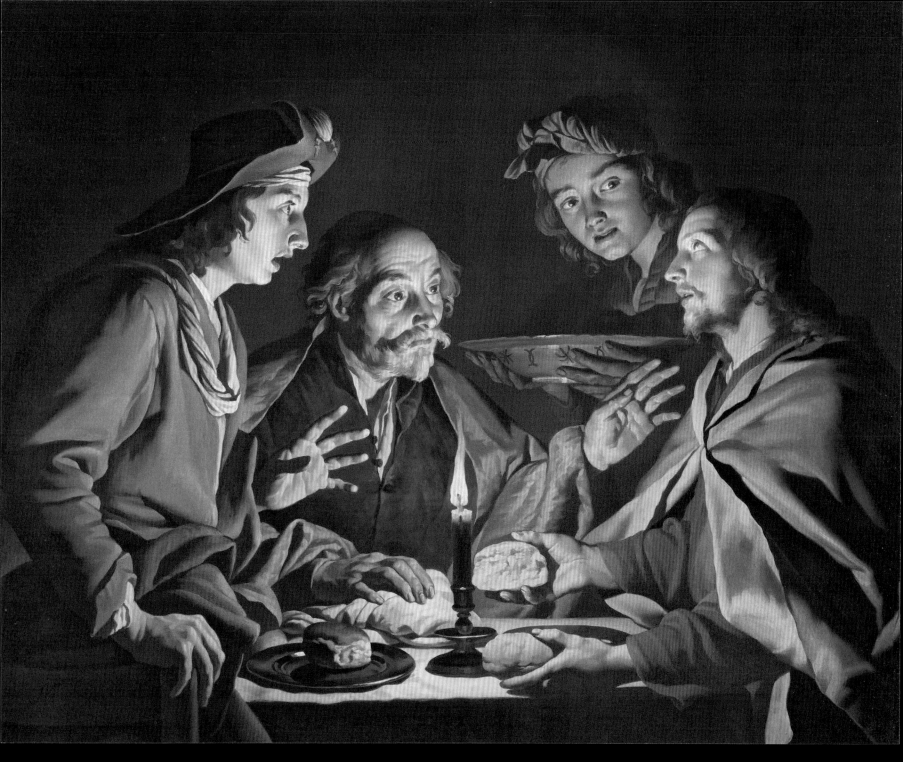

8.
The Supper at Emmaus

Matthias Stom, c. 1633–1639
Museo Nacional Thyssen-Bornemisza, Madrid

Light radiates from a single slender candle on a table set in a bare, darkened room. Piercing the cold darkness with radiant light, the candle flame warms the faces of three men huddled over the table, which is covered in plain linen and graced only by a plate of meat. A playful dog seeks the attention of the bearded man on the left, while a boy on the right, plate in hand, pauses in rapt attention to listen in. The room and the table may be simple, but this is no ordinary meal. It is the supper at Emmaus, shared by the Risen Jesus and two disciples after their long walk together.

Matthias Stom was a gifted seventeenth-century Dutch painter of biblical scenes who worked mostly in Italy. He sets this Gospel scene in a darkened room to allow his brilliant use of chiaroscuro — an artistic technique of using sharp contrasts of light and shadow to create a dramatic effect — to express the spiritual intensity of the moment. Caravaggio, the famed Italian Baroque painter, perfected this painting technique, and artists across Europe, such as Stom, were eager to imitate the master of chiaroscuro.

As we reflect on Stom's visual homily, we step into the story of this extraordinary meal at Emmaus. Into the darkness of the evening hour the disciples carry their physical exhaustion from their long walk. They also bring to the table, in their minds and hearts, their deep disappointment

As they approached the village to which they were going, [Jesus] gave the impression that he was going on farther. But they urged him, "Stay with us, for it is nearly evening and the day is almost over." So he went in to stay with them. And it happened that, while he was with them at the table, he took bread, said the blessing, broke it, and gave it to them. With that their eyes were opened and they recognized him, but he vanished from their sight. Then they said to each other, "Were not our hearts burning [within us] while he spoke to us on the way and opened the scriptures to us?"

Luke 24:28–32

and spiritual anguish over the suffering and death of Jesus, their Teacher and Lord. Saint Luke notes that they began their journey, both physical and spiritual, in the revered city of Jerusalem, the center of public worship and the site of Jesus' passion and his humiliating death by crucifixion. They were downcast as they talked about Jesus, the One foremost in their aching thoughts. Why were they downcast? Because the One they had believed, followed, and hoped in was no longer with them. The cross of Jesus was a defeat and an experience of abandonment they could not have imagined. They had left everything to follow Jesus, whose preaching and healing had revealed to them a divine power that made all things new. Jesus had transformed their lives. Now, like sheep without a shepherd, they felt only disorientation and emptiness.

Then, suddenly, there were no longer two but three people walking along the road to Emmaus. The stranger who walked with them was Jesus, but they could not recognize his resurrected body. Disappointment and fear clouded their vision. They informed the stranger with faint hope that they had heard that Jesus might be alive again:

"Some women from our group, however, have astounded us: they were at the tomb early in the morning and did not find his body; they came back and reported that they had indeed seen a vision of angels who announced that he was alive" (Lk 24:22–23).

After entering the heart of their conversation, Jesus began to interpret the Old Testament Scriptures — a kind of first Bible study group with a wise Teacher. The Word-made-flesh was unveiling the meaning of his own life, death, and resurrection in the revealed word of God. The disciples could understand how Jesus' life, death, and resurrection were the heart of the saving plan of the Creator to reconcile humanity to friendship with God. But even then, the disciples did not recognize that it was Jesus who walked and talked with them!

As their physical journey ended, the disciples extended an invitation to Jesus, urging him strongly, "Stay with us, for it is nearly evening and the

For in the mystery of the Word made flesh a new light of your glory has shone upon the eyes of our mind, so that, as we recognize in him God made visible, we may be caught up through him in love of things invisible.

Preface I, Nativity of the Lord, Christ the Light

VISIO DIVINA PRAYER

Jesus, open our eyes, physical and spiritual, to recognize your presence in the sacramental signs, gestures, and prayers of the Eucharist.

What material food produces in our bodily life, Holy Communion wonderfully achieves in our spiritual life. Communion with the flesh of the risen Christ, a flesh "given life and giving life through the Holy Spirit," preserves, increases, and renews the life of grace received at Baptism. (*Catechism of the Catholic Church*, 1392)

day is almost over" (Lk 24:29). Could it be that the disciples urged Jesus to stay because his words stirred new hope in them? They yearned to be close to the One who alone satisfies the deepest longings of the human heart — just as we do! The disciples' spiritual journey was about to deepen, for Jesus accepted their invitation. And what happened next at the table at Emmaus changed everything again, transforming the two disciples and, with them, the Church.

Matthias Stom tells the rest of the story in color, line, and light. We see Jesus with broken bread, a piece held in each hand. His eyes look up to heaven in a gesture of blessing as his serene face, illuminated by the candle, rivets the eyes of the disciples and the boy. Their eyes direct our gaze to Jesus. The warm light evokes the spiritual illumination of the moment: The light of God's love dispels the world's darkness.

Only a few days earlier, Jesus had taken, blessed, and broken bread at the Last Supper, when he instituted the sacred meal of the Eucharist as a foretaste of his passion and death on the cross. Stom captures for us this dramatic moment of "Eucharistic amazement" as the disciples raise their hands in astonished recognition of Jesus in the breaking of the bread. Their journey to Emmaus was a pilgrimage, through word and sacrament, of faith in the abiding presence of Jesus with them. This is the same presence that continues in the Church in every age and place, for every Mass, with its liturgy of the word and liturgy of the Eucharist, invites us to the same table of the Lord, where our hearts burn in the sacred presence of Jesus. And our communion with the Body and Blood of Jesus deepens the graces we received at our baptism.

Notice how the scene opens into our space with an empty place at the table. The artist invites us to take our place at the table of the Lord, who desires to stay with us and to nourish us with his own divine life and love as we make our way on the path of life.

9.

Disputation over the Holy Sacrament

Raphael, c. 1509–1510
Vatican Museums

The Eucharist unites heaven and earth, for "in the earthly liturgy we share in a foretaste of [the] heavenly liturgy" (CCC 1090). A sweeping vision of the heavenly and earthly realms with the Eucharist at the center is brought to life in *Disputation over the Holy Sacrament*, a magnificent fresco painted by Raphael, renowned master artist of the Italian High Renaissance. The glorious scene, completed between 1509 and 1510, adorns the walls of the Stanza della Segnatura. This richly adorned space is one of four Raphael Rooms in the Vatican's apostolic palace painted with depictions of the disciplines of philosophy, poetry, theology, and law. Pope Julius II once used the room (named for the highest court of the Vatican: the Segnatura Gratiae et Iustitiae) as a library and private office. On the opposite wall, Raphael's stunning fresco *School of Athens* gathers classical philosophers in a spirited debate. Another one of Raphael's masterpieces on the Eucharist painted in these remarkable Vatican rooms will be the focus of a later reflection.

In *Disputation over the Holy Sacrament*, completed when Raphael was twenty-seven, we see the Eucharist as the focal point of a vast heavenly and earthly assembly of biblical figures, saints of the Church, popes, and theo-

logians. As we gaze on the scene, we join, for a moment, in their Eucharistic amazement.

The vision unfolds in an arched, apse-like, semicircular space in which two groups, one in heaven and one on earth, are suspended in adoration before the mystery of the Eucharist. God the Father, depicted as a bearded old man, occupies the heavenly realm, arrayed in golden shafts of light. God extends his right hand in a gesture of blessing while holding a sphere, a symbol of the earth, in his left hand. Below, the resurrected Jesus sits on a throne of clouds, framed in a golden orb surrounded by angels. Jesus' face is serene and gentle as he stretches out his hands to display the wounds of his passion and death. At his side are Mary, his mother, and John the Baptist. The trio are flanked by a curving row of alternating Old Testament patriarchs, kings, and saints of the Church. These celestial figures float effortlessly on a thin layer of clouds held up by tiny cherubs. Reading the group from left to right, we see Saint Peter, Adam, St. John the Evangelist, David, Saint Lawrence, an unidentified saint, Judas Maccabeus, Saint Stephen, Moses, Saint James the Elder, Abraham, and Saint Paul.

The entire composition is a visual exaltation of the Blessed Trinity, with golden orbs that highlight and connect God the Father, God the Son, and God the Holy Spirit. The Holy Spirit, the love between the Father and the Son,

The cup of blessing that we bless, is it not a participation in the blood of Christ? The bread that we break, is it not a participation in the body of Christ? Because the loaf of bread is one, we, though many, are one body, for we all partake of the one loaf.

1 Corinthians 10:16–17

In humble prayer we ask you, almighty God: command that these gifts be borne by the hands of your holy Angel to your altar on high in the sight of your divine majesty, so that all of us, who through this participation at the altar receive the most holy Body and Blood of your Son, may be filled with every grace and heavenly blessing. Through Christ our Lord. Amen.

Eucharistic Prayer
I, Epiclesis

is represented by the traditional artistic symbol of a white dove. Overflowing from the Blessed Trinity, rays of golden light shine down from the Holy Spirit onto the Eucharist below, held in a monstrance on a richly decorated altar in the ethereal space that spans heaven and earth. This is a reminder that the transformation of bread and wine into the Body and Blood of Jesus in the Eucharist is the work of the Holy Spirit. The four Gospels, held up by cherubs, radiate from the inspiration of the Holy Spirit as well.

In the earthly realm, figures on either side of the altar discuss, in awe and wonder, the meaning of the Eucharist. Among them are Pope Julius II and the fiery Dominican preacher Savonarola. Seated on elegant marble thrones close to the altar are the four Fathers of the Latin Church — namely, St. Gregory the Great, Saint Jerome, Saint Ambrose, and Saint Augustine. The artist places the towering frame of Pope Sixtus IV, robed in vibrant gold papal vestments, on the lower right. Directly behind him stands the beloved poet Dante Alighieri, clothed in red and crowned with a laurel wreath. On the far opposite side, the Dominican friar artist Fra Angelico gazes at the Eucharist while a bald figure,

thought to be the famed Renaissance architect Bramante, reads a book as he leans over the railing.

In Scripture, remembering is not a mere recollection of past events but the proclamation of the mighty works of God in human history. In the liturgical celebrations of the Church, past events become present through the remembrance of God's mighty deeds and words. The people of Israel understood that their celebration of the Passover made the saving events of Exodus present in their memory so that they might conform their lives to them. In the New Testament, the remembering of Jesus' life, death, and resurrection takes on new meaning, transcending time and place. When the Church celebrates the Eucharist, the Passover of Jesus is made present, in the here and now, for us. In this way, the sacrifice of Jesus on the cross, offered once for all, remains ever present so we may experience its liberating grace.

Each of Raphael's figures represents the communion of the Church, in the heavenly communion of saints and in the community on earth, now gathered to share with one another their Eucharistic amazement. Time and space, heaven and earth, revolve around the Church's celebration of the Eucharist, "source and summit of the Christian life" (*Lumen Gentium*, par. 11). In the Eucharist, past, present, and future dissolve in the unity of the community of the Church across the ages. Raphael's painting reminds us that Jesus, whose sacrifice on the cross is re-presented at every Mass in the present age of the Church, will return in glory at the end of time to "judge the living and the dead," as we pray in the words of the Creed. The sacred feast of the Eucharist draws together past events in salvation history, which are fulfilled in the Paschal Mystery of Jesus' death and resurrection; the present participation of the community in its saving effects that transform the world; and the future hope of the heavenly liturgy in the company of the Blessed Trinity, Mary, the angels, and the saints.

VISIO DIVINA **PRAYER**

Lord, grant us the gifts of faith and hope, that our participation in the earthly Eucharist will unite us to the heavenly liturgy and allow us to grow in love of Jesus Christ, now and for all eternity.

There is no surer pledge or dearer sign of this great hope in the new heavens and new earth "in which righteousness dwells," than the Eucharist. Every time this mystery is celebrated, "the work of our redemption is carried on" and we "break the one bread that provides the medicine of immortality, the antidote for death, and the food that makes us live forever in Jesus Christ." (*Catechism of the Catholic Church*, 1405)

For I received from the Lord what I also handed on to you, that the Lord Jesus, on the night he was handed over, took bread, and, after he had given thanks, broke it and said, "This is my body that is for you. Do this in remembrance of me." In the same also the cup, after supper, saying, "This cup is the new covenant in my blood. Do this, as often as you drink it, in remembrance of me." For as often as you eat this bread and drink this cup, you proclaim the death of the Lord until he comes.

1 Corinthians 11:23–26

10.
Mass of Saint Gregory

Attributed to Diego de la Cruz, c. 1490
Philadelphia Museum of Art

Commonly known as Saint Gregory the Great, Pope Gregory I reigned from 590 to 604. The story of the beloved pope's dramatic Eucharistic vision, said to have occurred while he celebrated Mass, first emerged in an eighth-century papal biography by Paul the Deacon, a Benedictine historian. By the fourteenth century, various accounts of his vision had spread among the faithful and inspired many artistic renditions. This Spanish Renaissance painting, attributed to Diego de la Cruz, is one artist's dramatic depiction of the saintly pope's vision, in which the sacrifice of Jesus' passion and death on the cross is visually connected to the Mass. The painting is rendered in a unique aerial, close-up perspective, with the viewer seeming to hover above the profound vision unfolding at the altar.

We see Pope Gregory facing east and kneeling before an altar, on which can be seen a chalice, a paten with a cross design, and a sacramentary, the book of prayers said or sung by the priest at Mass. He is vested in a chasuble, richly embroidered with flowers, pearls, and ecclesial figures. To his left, a cardinal robed in red holds a papal tiara, a jeweled three-tiered ceremonial crown typically worn during papal coronations. The kneeling cardinal looks heavenward, imitating the pope's gaze. On the floor between them sits a vessel of holy water.

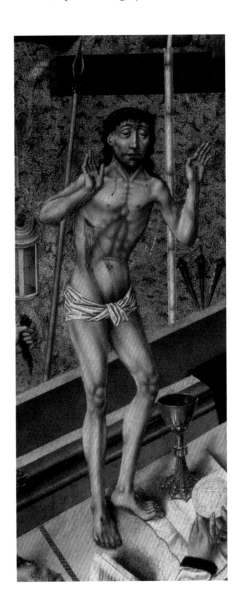

To the right, a tonsured monk is the altar server who lifts the pope's chasuble with his left hand while holding, in his right hand, a long rod topped with a lit candle, also known as the elevation candle. These two liturgical gestures indicate the sacred moment of the Mass when the priest elevates the consecrated Host. The lifting of the chasuble relieved some of the weight of the priest's vestments, allowing him to give the highest elevation to the Host so that the faithful behind him could see it. Before the advent of electricity, an elevation candle allowed the faithful to see the Host and the chalice, elevated in dimly lit churches. In this scene, Pope Gregory elevates a Host embossed with the cross of Jesus, leading our eye to the vision he sees over the altar.

As Pope Gregory elevates the Host, a vision of Jesus as the Man of Sorrows appears before him. Jesus stands on the altar with one foot on the corporal, the cloth under the chalice. Jesus' feet show bloody nail marks, and his raised arms reveal more nail marks on his blood-stained hands. His head is pierced with a crown of thorns, and his gaunt, bruised body bears an open wound from the lance that was thrust into his side. Blood from his wounded side streams into the ornate chalice on the altar.

Behind the suffering figure of Jesus, against a gold background, the artist has painted several visual reminders of the Passion. The column where

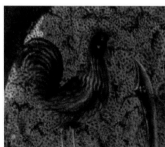

Jesus was scourged is topped by a rooster (or cock), the symbol of Peter's betrayal. A sword and an abstracted human ear recall Peter's hasty act of cutting off the ear of the high priest's servant when they came to arrest Jesus in the garden. On either side of the Lord's bloodied frame, we see the lance and the rod with the sponge dipped in vinegar, given as drink to Jesus. Three large nails appear next to the cross, on which are inscribed the letters INRI, the Latin acronym of the title given to him by Pilate: "Jesus, the Nazarene, King of the Jews." An abstracted image of a slapping hand, a metal instrument of torture, and the face of a man spitting at Jesus are painful re-

minders of the mockery and ridicule he endured during his Passion. We see Judas betraying Jesus with a kiss. Around Judas's neck hangs a large red moneybag, a symbol of the base greed and cowardice of his betrayal of Jesus for the "blood money" of thirty pieces of silver. A ladder leans against the cross. The empty tomb lies at the foot of the cross. On the far right of the painting, a tonsured monk kneels with hands folded in prayer. Above his head, a silver basin, a jug of water, and a towel remind us

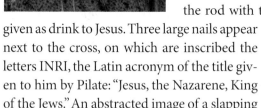

*Fulfilling your will
and gaining for you
a holy people,*

*he stretched out his hands
as he endured his Passion,*

*so as to break the bonds
of death and manifest
the resurrection.*

Eucharistic Prayer
II, Preface

VISIO DIVINA PRAYER

Jesus, may we recognize that you offered your redeeming sacrifice on the cross, celebrated in the Eucharist, out of the fullness of your divine love so that we might become a new creation in you.

When the Church celebrates the Eucharist, she commemorates Christ's Passover, and it is made present: the sacrifice Christ offered once for all on the cross remains ever present. "As often as the sacrifice of the Cross by which 'Christ our Pasch has been sacrificed' is celebrated on the altar, the work of our redemption is carried out." (*Catechism of the Catholic Church*, 1364)

of Jesus' humble act of servant-like love as he washed the feet of his disciples the night before his passion.

Pope Gregory's unusually vivid vision, recorded in papal biographies and depicted in artistic works, visibly connects the divine love revealed in the passion of Jesus with the Mass, which is its memorial. This masterpiece recalls the *Catechism*'s teaching that since Christ was about to take his departure from his own in his visible form, he wanted to give us his sacramental presence; since he was about to offer himself on the cross to save us, he wanted us to have the memorial of the love with which he loved us "to the end," even to the giving of his life. In his Eucharistic presence, he remains mysteriously in our midst as the one who loved us and gave himself up for us, and he remains under signs that express and communicate this love (see 1380).

The unique aerial perspective the artist uses in his image reminds us of the divine love revealed in the physical and emotional sufferings that Jesus willingly endured to reconcile us to friendship with God. As we make this pilgrimage along the Way of Beauty toward a deeper appreciation of the Eucharistic feast, may we recognize Jesus' loving invitation to grow in union with him and in love of our neighbor. In the words of Pope St. John Paul II, "The Church and the world have a great need of Eucharistic worship. Jesus waits for us in this sacrament of love. Let us be generous with our time in going to meet Him in adoration and in contemplation that is full of faith and ready to make reparation for the great faults and crimes of the world. Let our adoration never cease" (*Dominicae Cenae*, par. 3).

11.
The Mass at Bolsena

Raphael, c. 1512–1514
Vatican Museums

In the interior recesses of the Vatican's vast apostolic palace, the official residence of popes since the sixteenth century, one can view a dramatic series of frescoes by the Italian Renaissance artist Raffaello Sanzio da Urbino, known to the world as Raphael. In an earlier reflection, we explored one of these masterpieces: *Disputation over the Holy Sacrament*. Along with Michelangelo and Leonardo da Vinci, Raphael is celebrated as one of the master artists of the High Renaissance. This fresco, titled *The Mass at Bolsena* and completed between 1512 and 1514, gives evidence of Raphael's unparalleled artistic genius. Painted in a lunette above a massive window in the Stanza di Eliodoro, this work depicts a Eucharistic miracle believed to have taken place in Bolsena, Italy.

Reading the painting from left to right, we see a crowd of faithful men, women, and children facing the altar as they fix their gaze on the miracle unfolding before them. With hands folded in prayer or raised in a gesture of praise to God, they direct our gaze to the center of the composition. High above this worshiping group are two men behind a railing, one of whom gestures to the other, who is pointing animatedly to the altar with his left hand.

Young altar servers dressed in white hold aloft three large candles. We can

almost see those candles flicker with the golden light that illumines the altar, on which are placed two large candles, a crucifix, and two chalices. A kneeling altar server gently lifts the priest's chasuble, the outermost liturgical garment, which is trimmed with an ornate laurel wreath pattern that leads our eye up to the altar, where the Eucharistic miracle unfolds.

So they said to him, "Sir, give us this bread always." Jesus said to them, "I am the bread of life; whoever comes to me will never hunger, and whoever believes in me will never thirst."

John 6:34–35

According to legend, the miracle took place in 1263 in the Church of Santa Cristina in Bolsena. There, a priest who was celebrating Mass harbored doubts about the Church's doctrine of transubstantiation, the change in the substances of the bread and wine into the Body and Blood of Jesus. Soon, the priest noticed blood on the consecrated Host. The miraculous blood fell from the Host onto the corporal — the cloth on which the chalice and paten are placed on the altar — in the shape of a cross. Raphael captures the moment when the priest is caught up in this miraculous event, freed from his doubts about the sacramental presence of Jesus' Body and Blood under the appearances of bread and wine. To this day, the blood-stained corporal is venerated as a relic in Bolsena and is central to the elaborate Corpus Christi processions celebrated there each year.

Kneeling in front of the altar as a witness to this Eucharistic miracle is Pope Julius II, who reigned from 1503 to 1513. Behind the pope, on the right

Be pleased, O God, we pray, to bless, acknowledge, and approve this offering in every respect; make it spiritual and acceptable, so that it may become for us the Body and Blood of your most beloved Son, our Lord Jesus Christ.

Eucharistic Prayer I, Epiclesis

side of the painting, Raphael has painted four cardinals who were papal relatives. Finally, in a subtle expression of his own faith in the Eucharist, Raphael has included a portrait of himself as one of five richly dressed Swiss Guards located in the lower right of the fresco. Raphael is the figure clothed in red with bound-up hair, who looks out directly at the viewer as if to invite our faith in the gift and mystery of the Eucharist.

The Eucharistic Prayer is the heart of the Liturgy of the Eucharist. At the center of the Eucharistic Prayer is the *epiclesis.* At that moment, the Church prays to the Father, asking for the power of the Holy Spirit to make the Eucharistic elements of bread and wine into the Body and

Blood of Jesus Christ. The movement of the Holy Spirit on the elements of bread and wine overflows onto the assembly so that all those gathered in the name of Jesus become what they receive: one body and one spirit in Jesus Christ. This sacred moment is a true miracle!

The *Catechism*'s glossary describes a miracle as "a sign or wonder, such as a healing or the control of nature, which can only be attributed to divine power." In the Eucharist, Christ is "really and mysteriously made *present*" (CCC 1357), and his sacramental presence is the Church's daily miracle by which we participate in the very life and love of God.

VISIO DIVINA PRAYER

Jesus, grant that the miracle of every Eucharist may lead us from the visible to the invisible, from the signs to the abundant graces signified, and from the sacrament to the mystery of your real and living presence in the Church.

That in this sacrament are the true Body of Christ and his true Blood is something that "cannot be apprehended by the senses," says St. Thomas, "but *only by faith*, which relies on divine authority." For this reason, in a commentary on Luke 22:19 ("This is my body which is given for you."), St. Cyril says: "Do not doubt whether this is true, but rather receive the words of the Savior in faith, for since he is the truth, he cannot lie." (*Catechism of the Catholic Church*, 1381)

12.

The Virgin Adoring the Host

Jean-Auguste-Dominique Ingres, c. 1852
Metropolitan Museum of Art, New York

As the mother of Jesus, Mary was one of the first to gaze on the face of her divine Son. At the Annunciation, Mary was overshadowed by the Holy Spirit and responded to the Archangel Gabriel with her yes to God's call to bear his Son into the world. In her Magnificat, Mary sang praise for the divine love and mercy that was reconciling humanity to friendship with God. At Jesus' birth, Mary joined the chorus of angels in glorifying God for the wonder of the Incarnation. With Joseph, and in the company of the shepherds and the three wise men, Mary revered the Word-made-Flesh in silent adoration before his sacred presence. Throughout his public ministry, Mary witnessed Jesus' love for the poor and his signs, miracles, and healings as the unveiling of God's reign on earth. At Calvary, Mary shared uniquely, as his mother, in her son's suffering and death on the cross. After the Resurrection and the Ascension, Mary waited in joyful hope for the gift of the Holy Spirit at Pentecost.

Mary "lived her *Eucharistic faith* even before the institution of the Eucharist" because she bore in her own Body the body of Christ, which she brought into the world (*Ecclesia de Eucharistia*, par. 55). Mary is, as Pope John Paul II noted, a "'woman of the Eucharist' in her whole life" (par. 53). It is this unique relationship of Mary to the Eucharist, to the Church, and to the faithful that

And Mary kept all these things, reflecting on them in her heart.

Luke 2:19

the French painter Jean-Auguste-Dominique Ingres evokes in this striking masterpiece. Titled *The Virgin Adoring the Host*, the small devotional painting was completed around 1852 as a gift for a friend. In his ethereal vision, Ingres imagines Mary praying before the sacred Host in the presence of two saints. The work reminds us that Mary intercedes always for us, and it invites us to join Mary as she contemplates the Eucharistic presence of Jesus, her divine Son.

We see three tightly grouped figures before a semicircular, apse-like wall framed by two large columns. Two lit candlesticks are placed on either end of a bare stone altar, on which the Host is placed atop a golden chalice and paten. The stately figure on the left is Saint Helena, mother of the fourth-century emperor Constantine. This saintly woman is believed to have discovered the true cross of Jesus during her pilgrimage to Jerusalem. Saint Helena's haloed head bears a large golden crown with precious stones that mirror the ornate decoration on her regal robe. She looks intently at the Blessed Virgin Mary while grasping the upright of the cross in her right hand.

On the right stands the saintly French king Louis IX, draped in a deep-blue velvet robe studded with golden fleurs-de-lis, traditional symbols of Mary and long used by French royalty as signs of the nation's sovereignty. A golden fleur-de-lis can also be seen at the top of the royal staff he bears in his right hand. He holds his ornate crown in his left hand, and his eyes direct our gaze to the Host at the center of the painting. Engraved on the Host are a cross and the letters IHS, a monogram of the first three letters of the name of Jesus in Greek.

In the foreground and bathed in radiant light is the serene figure of Mary, clothed in a red garment and a deep-blue silk robe draped over her haloed head. Her blue and red garments symbolize the divinity and humanity of her divine Son. Her slender fingers come together in prayer as her luminous, youthful face turns gently to the altar in a gesture of prayerful adoration. Her eyes gaze downward at the sacred Host as she prays in the Eucharistic presence of Jesus.

Tota pulchra es ("You are totally beautiful") is a fourth-century prayer honoring and reverencing the Blessed Virgin Mary. The hymn praises Mary as being "totally beautiful" because she is the only creature whom God preserved from the stain of original sin so that she could bear his divine Son into the world. With this in mind, we find in Mary an especially trusted pilgrimage companion on the Way of Beauty. Through the eyes of his mother, we encounter Jesus in the Eucharist.

At the end of his earthly existence, Jesus assured his disciples that he would remain with them: "And behold, I am with you always, until the end of the age" (Mt 28:20). Jesus' earthly life and ministry did not end with his ascension into heaven. In the age of the Church, his saving and real presence continues in the liturgy, most especially in the Eucharist.

The Second Vatican Council teaches that Jesus is present in the community of the Church in manifold ways. He is present in the priest, who acts in the person of Christ, the head of his Body, the Church (*in persona Christi capitis*). He is present in the Eucharistic species of bread and wine that become

*May he make of us an
eternal offering to you,
so that we may obtain*

*an inheritance with your
elect, especially with
the most Blessed Virgin
Mary, Mother of God,*

*with blessed Joseph,
her Spouse,*

*with your blessed Apostles
and glorious Martyrs
and with all the Saints,*

*on whose constant
intercession in your
presence, we rely for
unfailing help.*

Eucharistic Prayer
III, Intercessions

his Body and Blood in the memorial of the Eucharist. He is present in Sacred Scripture, his word proclaimed and lived out by the community of believers. And he is present where two or three gather in his name, which includes the assembly at worship.

Pope John Paul II observed that the mystery of the Eucharist — sacrifice, presence, banquet — *does not allow for reduction or exploitation*; it must be experienced and lived in its integrity, both in its celebration and in the intimate conversation with Jesus which takes place after receiving communion or in a prayerful moment of Eucharistic adoration apart from Mass. These are times when the Church is firmly built up and it becomes clear what she truly is: one, holy, catholic, and apostolic; the people, temple and family of God; the body and bride of Christ, enlivened by the Holy Spirit; the universal sacrament of salvation and a hierarchically structured communion. (*Ecclesia de Eucharistia*, par. 61)

When we accept God's invitation to the sacred feast of the Eucharist, we follow in the footsteps of the Blessed Virgin Mary, the "woman of the Eucharist." She is the "first tabernacle of the New Covenant," and her yes to the Archangel Gabriel echoes in our amen as we receive the Body and Blood of Christ in the Eucharist. We are welcomed by Christ at his table of word and sacrament; we receive his divine forgiveness, spiritual strength, and healing; we are nourished by his word and his bread; and we are sent on mission into the world. There, we bear witness to our Eucharistic encounter with Jesus by our words and deeds so that, through us, his sacred presence may transform the world. The Eucharist strengthens our hope that, in Jesus, human suffering and pain will be transfigured as we pass, with him, from life to death to new life. Offering to Jesus, the Bread of Life, our lives, our families, our work, and all of creation, we glimpse a foretaste of the eternal, heavenly banquet, the goal of our worship and life. To that future sacred feast, in the presence of the Father, the Son, and the Holy Spirit, in the company of the Blessed Virgin Mary, the angels and saints, and the communion of the Church, we have also been invited.

VISIO DIVINA PRAYER

Blessed Mother Mary, may our amen to the Body and Blood of Christ lead us closer to you, *tota pulchra*, the most beautiful of God's creatures. Lead us always to your divine Son, Jesus, the Word-made-Flesh in your womb, the same Jesus who desires to dwell in us in the Eucharist.

In the liturgy of the Mass we express our faith in the real presence of Christ under the species of bread and wine by, among other ways, genuflecting or bowing deeply as a sign of adoration of the Lord. "The Catholic Church has always offered and still offers to the sacrament of the Eucharist the cult of adoration, not only during Mass, but also outside of it, reserving the consecrated hosts with the utmost care, exposing them to the solemn veneration of the faithful, and carrying them in procession."

(*Catechism of the Catholic Church*, 1378)

Tantum Ergo Sacramentum

Eucharistic hymn of St. Thomas Aquinas

Tantum ergo Sacraméntum
Venerémur cérnui:
Et antíquum documéntum
Novo cedat rítui:
Praestet fides suppleméntum
Sénsuum deféctui.

Genitóri, Genitóque
Laus et jubilátio,
Salus, honor, virtus quoque
Sit et benedíctio:
Procedénti ab utróque
Compar sit laudátio. Amen.

Down in adoration falling,
This great sacrament we hail;
Over ancient forms of worship
Newer rites of grace prevail;
Faith will tell us Christ is present,
When our human senses fail.

To the everlasting Father,
And the Son who made us free,
And the Spirit, God proceeding
From them each eternally,
Be salvation, honor, blessing,
Might and endless majesty. Amen.

Artwork Credits

1. Artist unknown, *Sacrifice of Abel and Melchizedek*, c. 538–545, mosaic, Basilica of San Vitale, Ravenna, Italy, Bridgeman Images.
2. Sir Peter Paul Rubens, *The Meeting of Abraham and Melchizedek*, c. 1626, oil on panel, National Gallery of Art, Washington, D.C.
3. Follower of Peter Coecke van Elst, *The Gathering of Manna*, c. 1532–1535, tempera on panel, Philadelphia Museum of Art, Philadelphia.
4. Artist unknown, Spanish, *The Holy Family at Table*, seventeenth century, oil on canvas, Philadelphia Museum of Art, Philadelphia.
5. Bartolomé Esteban Murillo, *The Marriage Feast at Cana*, c. 1672, oil on canvas, The Barber Institute of Fine Arts, Birmingham, UK.
6. Bartolomé Esteban Murillo, *The Parable of the Prodigal Son*, c. 1667–1670, oil on canvas, National Gallery of Art, Washington, D.C.
7. Juan de Juanes, *The Last Supper*, c. 1562, oil on panel, Museo del Prado, Madrid.
8. Matthias Stom, *The Supper at Emmaus*, c. 1633–1639, oil on canvas, Museo Nacional Thyssen-Bornemisza, Madrid.
9. Raphael, *Disputation over the Most Holy Sacrament*, c. 1509–1510, fresco, Vatican Museums, Vatican City.
10. Attributed to Diego de la Cruz, *Mass of Saint Gregory*, c. 1490, oil and gold on panel, Philadelphia Museum of Art, Philadelphia.
11. Raphael, *The Mass at Bolsena*, c. 1512–1514, fresco, Vatican Museums, Vatican City.
12. Jean-Auguste-Dominique Ingres, *The Virgin Adoring the Host*, c. 1852, oil on canvas, Metropolitan Museum of Art, New York.

About the Author

Dr. Jem Sullivan is associate professor of catechetics in the School of Theology and Religious Studies at the Catholic University of America, Washington, D.C. She is an appointed member of the International Council for Catechesis in the Dicastery for Evangelization in Rome. Dr. Sullivan has served the Church's catechetical initiatives at the international, national, diocesan, and parish levels and has educated graduate and undergraduate students for more than two decades. She has served as a volunteer art-museum docent and is the author of five books, including a book on the place of the arts in evangelization and catechesis.

You might also like:

The Beauty of Faith:
Using Christian Art to Spread the Good News
By Jem Sullivan, Ph.D.

Over 2,000 years, Christian art has expressed the truth of the Catholic Faith for generations of the faithful. Learn the language of art to make visible the mysteries of Scripture and traditions through paintings, sculpture, mosaics, stained glass, poetry, and sacred music.

Discover art as a visual Gospel that can guide, nourish, and strengthen our daily witness to the Gospel today.

Available at
OSVCatholicBookstore.com
or wherever books are sold

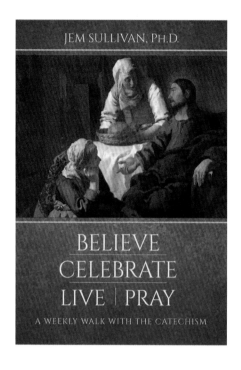